for.

Su:

Just because I
"Let It Happen"
I walked into the
Ventura Bookstore
at the "Marina" — 2 days ago.
First book I picked
up (this was it) I knew
I should send it
to you.

Love Pam

Albert Krassner

Let it just happen

Albert Krassner

Let it just happen

todays and yesterdays haiku

Veridon Editions

$4.95
ISBN 0-912061-08-1
Copyright 1986 by Albert Krassner
Graphic design: arcoiris/México
Veridon Editions
Box 65, Wykagyl Station
New Rochelle, NY 10804
USA

Dedication

To the Creative Energy
that manifests in infinite forms,
at all times,
in all places.

Foreword

Let it just happen is the first book
in a series presenting two forms of expression,
verbal and pictorial, associated together.
The words are written in a special structure
of ancient Japanese poetry, **haiku.**
The structure calls for seventeen syllables
in three lines of five, seven and five, respectively.
Rather than restrict, the form invites imagination to expand the communication.
The thoughts are those of a Western man
expressing his searchings, findings and feelings
living in contemporary American society.
The pictorial form is made up by a selection of distinctive designs,
simple, delicate symbolic expressions, created by a number of
medieval Japanese artists who were called on to identify friend or foe
in warring times by distinctive drawings suggesting various subject matter.
Both expressions deal with nature, human relationships, love, sharing, giving,
peace and harmony and awareness of more than what is seen with the eye.
Joined together they enhance the communication beyond
what each form does standing alone.
The editing and design team of "arcoiris" of Guadalajara, Mexico
was responsible for the selection, editing and presentation
of the contents in the books of the series.

Let it just happen.
Whatever will be will be,
The present controls.

For a happy life
Seek wisdom and perspective...
Find a true teacher.

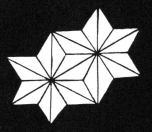

Living is precious.
To be open, receptive,
To receive and give.

Biblical gleanings.
History repeats itself,
History teaches.

Holding pure motive.
Keeping an eye on the truth –
Not easy to do.

Infinite supply.
Goodness, kindness, compassion...
No need to measure.

Human frailty.
Life cannot be understood,
Only accepted.

Night symphony.
Incessant sounds in single key –
Katydids chorus.

Breezes in the trees
Lightly lifting leaves on bough —
Soft white light shines forth.

Fall flowers unfurled
Assorted colors in bloom –
Stops one in his tracks.

Clear, cool, windless air...
Sun shining in a blue sky...
Made to order day.

Flower arranging–
Nature's colors always blend...
It doesn't matter.

Enriching the soul
Yellow, purple, red, orange...
Chrysanthemums.

Doing what one can –
Feeling light, accepting, giving...
Living the moment.

Cultivate the mind...
At all times loving, giving.
Harvest contentment.

Love, goodness, kindness...
Common denominators –
Indivisible.

The heart swells with joy...
Nothingness pervades the mind,
It is something new.

For freedom to be
Continuous surrender.
No contradiction.

Love for another
Projecting what is within
Cannot be contained.

To live happily
Be true to oneself – don't lie.
Sage words of advice.

Focus on God's love
As one does for daily bread...
Sustains, nourishes.

Coming together –
All is one under the sun.
The universe too.

Miracle of birth
Bringing joys beyond compare.
Continuity.

Whatever one does,
Focus be fully absorbed...
Enjoyment follows.

Accepting one's fate
While striving to affect it...
Human dilemma.

Myths, self-images
Can exaggerate, mislead...
Powerful forces.

Let go of the past
Tomorrow cannot be known...
This moment is sure.

To do or not do,
Searching, evaluating,
Questioning who does...

To challenge oneself
Brings surprises, delights, growth
Only for humans.

Challenges always
In different forms for all
As long as one lives.

Seeing the Big Play
Accepting one's part as is...
Seeking this blessing.

Touching another
In a way which cannot be seen...
Inner sensation.

Going openly
Aware of the potential...
Easy and detached.

Unconditional...
Love expressed to one's fellow –
Nothing in exchange.

Purpose in living
Doing for self, others too...
Self discovery.

Each moment forever
Never to return never.
Love it...however.

Watching all thoughts
Letting go of negative ones...
Continuous process.

Becoming upset
Losing equilibrium
Mind out of control.

Directing one's thoughts
Not letting them run rampant.
Privilege of man.

Appearing crazy
Said of many great beings...
Only time can tell.

Quieting the mind
Feeling the ease that follows...
Letting it go on

Confusion abounds
Frustration is everywhere.
The inner sun shines.

Submerge ego-pride
See all as the greater Self...
Freedom does result.

God's supremacy
Life giving and life taking...
Ferocious and calm.

No agitation.
Peace and tranquility.
The Ultimate State.

Feeling religious
Unbending, unshakable...
Keeps one together.

No easy answers
Always discrimination.
Truth is always felt.

There is nothing else
Nothing outside of oneself
Just to be oneself.

Total absorption.
No distraction whatever.
True meditation.

Facing life bravely...
Confident that all is well,
Each day a new start.

Sensing inner light
Feeling more inside
A place of pure love.

Never forgetting
Recognizing all is God...
Whatever it is.

Come play in my world
It is a wonderful place.
Do your everything.

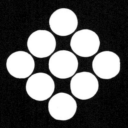

Incomparable
Living spiritually...
Infinite pathways.

Living the moment
Accepting all graciously.
Going with pure love.

Never arrogance –
It's not our Play anyway.
Useless energy.

Great power within.
Meditate daily.
Experience bliss.

Cultivate the mind.
Let only beauty flourish.
Weed out harmful thought.

Keeping one's focus
Reflecting on the Essence.
Man is not in charge.

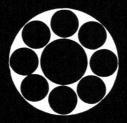

The Temple of Love
To find contentment and joy
Inside everyone.

Sages from the past
Have left wisdom for all men.
No greater treasure.

Perceiving the Truth
Remembering it all times
Never more in doubt.

Be in the moment
Fully, without sentiment.
Have eternity.

Devotion to God
Based on an Experience.
Forever lasting.

Poetry by Albert Krassner,
age **61**, American, born in New York City,
with a family of five children, one grandchild,
and currently living in New Rochelle, NY.
Professionally a lawyer and CPA,
he is a man of varied pursuits including flying his own airplane.
He started writing poetry six years ago
and is the author of **Journey to be**, **Notations Through Verse**,
Untrampled Ground, and other works.